REFLECTIONS

A BOOK OF POEMS

ITAI DAVID NJANJI

ISBN (Paperback): 978-0-578-39049-9
ISBN (eBook): 978-0-578-39050-5

Library of Congress Control Number: 2022934756

All content reflects our opinion at a given time and
can change as time progresses. All information should be
taken as an opinion and should not be misconstrued
for professional or legal advice. The contents of this
book are informational in nature and are not legal or tax
advice, and the authors and publishers are not engaged
in the provision of legal, tax, or any other advice.

Cover and interior layout design by Jess LaGreca

Printed in the United States of America

First printing edition 2022

www.ItaiDavidNjanji.com

A BOOK OF POEMS

Growing up in Africa,
Building a life in America, and
Traveling around the world.

I dedicate this book to my family and friends,
who have loved me unconditionally.

TABLE OF CONTENTS

FAITH

The only thing I ever had was faith
Somehow, I found it at a young age.
Born into poverty,
Father was born in Mozambique,
Mother in Zimbabwe,
Family settled in South Africa.
Father died when I was 10
Mother when I was 18
Uncles and Aunts raised me.
Yet I lacked nothing
I had no money
But slept and laughed.
A cricket scholarship sent me to school
Another to College.
Many were qualified but yet I prospered
I was the first son of the third wife: nothing to aspire for
Terrible Odds!
Remember how they forgot David?
Maybe that was why my mother named me Itai David
Faith carried me across the Atlantic
How did I ever come to this place?
The inexplicable happened
Wall Street
Big Tech
Travel
Love
I am not the most deserving
Neither very tall nor best looking
The brightest nor the most groomed
The hardest working nor shrewdest

When you come so far, it's easy to forget
But in these poems, I remember
In the end
The only thing I will ever have is faith.

SECTION ONE

GROWING UP IN AFRICA

WHEN I WAS BORN

As a child, I hated where I was born!
Sun bright and orange, dazzling the sky.

From the Zambezi to Limpopo
A scourge on a foreigner's pale skin.

Nature prepared me for this sun
Brown eyes and dark skin.

Nature prepared me for this sun
The delicious maize and mango in an old farm,

Owned by an old settler
Plunder!

Books were the only remedy to my poverty,
Somewhere in this humble house my mother owned.

First son of the third wife
But nature prepared me for this role.

Stubborn and rude to destiny
So, I built my own house of stone.

Book by book, I built the foundation.
Lured away, I left my home for a house of plastic
Somewhere in America.

Home is where I am enough
A cause for gratitude,

Giving without expectations
Receiving and sharing,

Home is where I am accepted
Crying and laughing.

Lesson learned
When I die, I will love where I die!

94 MUPINI DRIVE

Last night I had a nightmare.
I gasped and panted, and my heart pumped.
Someone had sold my mother's house.
I couldn't remember who, but had my usual suspects:
My father's younger wife, his brother and my half-brothers.
Behind my back they had forged the papers and become
    owners.
I don't blame them; I have been away so long;
Stranger in my own country.
Many times, I had expressed my dislike of it:
Dirty walls, broken windows, and a plague of cultural wars.

But this time I went ballistic, exploded like a beast
unleashed.
Waved a cricket bat at my father's younger wife.
She blamed my father's brother, or attempted to . . .
In reality, I was kind and generous to both.
Never inherited hate.
But in the dream, I threatened to destroy everyone, and
    to sue.
To sue? Who? In Africa?
Another American influence in my dream.
Truth be told, I could afford another house, bigger, better.
But I wanted this one, only this one, this parched piece
    of land
In the middle of nowhere.
Someone had sold my house.

HOMESICK

Distance, you betrayed me.

How could I not remember my parents?
I lost my way

Walking aimlessly, seeking something
That already exists at home.

You made a stranger out of my sibling.
And a prodigal son out of me.

Homesickness is the price I pay for this life.

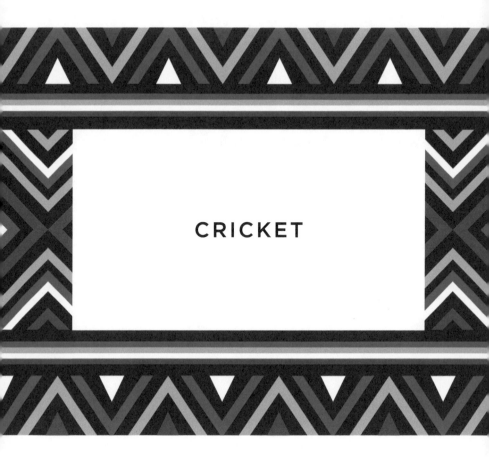

CRICKET

Cricket was my mother.
A mother I ran into!

By chance I found you,
Hidden in a ball in the ghetto.

Your milk was unnatural but nourishing.
By 13 your reach was far.

Scholarships!
A crown for an amateur career.

A feat my other mother noticed.
So, she let you adopt me!

I never appreciated you
Until that night,

You became my only mother.
The day my mother withered to death.

Cricket saved my life!

FAINA

Black Granite is the color of my mother's tombstone
Majestic like her character.

Every mined stone is broken
So was her life.

She was generous as she was kind
Pouring from an empty cup.

Generosity is what's left after giving
Nothing was left behind.

She was wise and uneducated
Is wisdom worth more than education?

Wisdom is good instincts in action.
Education is the greatest equalizer after God.

Never inherit hate
My mother was right.

Few friends are better than many
A hard lesson to learn.

A mother's hardship is a son's motivation
My inspiration.

She laughed and told good stories.
My happy memories.

Success begins the moment a mother is proud
Children are a parent's crown.

To a proud mother:
They stand tall like ancient Baobab trees
Roots deep.
Like Zulu warriors they conquer
And bloom like flowers in spring.

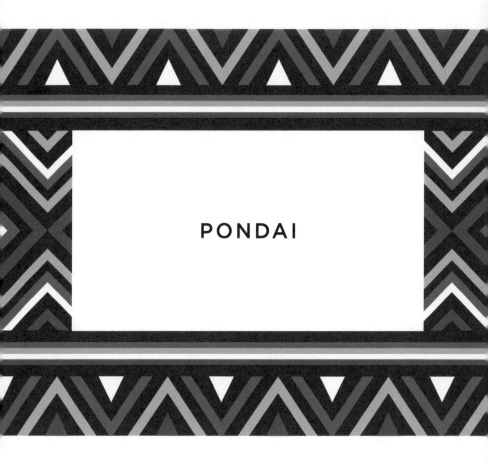

PONDAI

That night I lay silent in bed
A life put asunder,
Trapped in the cracks
Between New and Old.
Between Western and African.
Cracked open like a gourd.
Split Brain.
Witchcraft, goblins, and religion on my left.
Science and logic on my right.
Which one to choose?
Why does death bring more knowledge than life?
I told my siblings and half siblings that I liked him when
    I was young.
They told me I was poor, young, and liked everyone with
    money.
He loved and drank deeply.
I never said goodbye.
Solace can only be found in poems now.
That was the night my half-brother died.
The night Pondai died.

MOURNING

Scrapped of everything that we hold dear.
Hear us cry,

With no rye to drown our sorrows
No hope for consolation.

In Africa we would sing all night and drink rye
Africans mourn differently in America.

I met her during my sophomore year
She offered broad smiles with no reservations.

All Africans are related in America
It's an unspoken rule.

She was my African sister
That fateful accident took more than life:

Death of a young woman
Death of a breadwinner

Death of a first-generation college graduate
Death of an African in America.

Who sends her mother and sisters money now?
I haven't talked to our shared friend since her death.

It's 9 years and counting
No one ever taught us how to mourn our dead in
    a foreign land.

NOW

Trapped between the lies and the lives
Searching for the connecting light
Maybe, a line?

Dangling between a slice in time
A life in a framed portrait
Observed by a stranger's eyes

Simply a mere moment
A slice in time
What is now?

LOBOLA

Wheels on my brain and wheels on my motorcar
Wheeled off and smashed into the wall.
BAAM!
That is the sound of dissonance.
A fight broke
Brother-in-law, you dared not raise your voice!
Where is the Lobola for my sister?

SISTER

Never have I felt such pain
Inconceivable to my black male brain.

Born into a web of lies:
Lies about your race
Lies about your sex
What happened to the Queen of Sheba?

Never believe their lies.
Forever, remember I wrote these lines.

Open your eyes,
See!

Butterflies silently sing
Proteas and Daisies dance in the wind

While the African sun glows and illuminates
The beauty of a black woman.

PEACE OF MIND

Peace of mind
Is worth more than any other peace.

Like a comfortable house
Is peace of mind.

Walk freely, explore every room
No prisoners can be found,

Winds may batter it
Still the foundation stands.

Lose your peace of mind
Lose the world.

Gain your peace of mind
Gain more than the world.

Peace of mind
Is worth more than any other peace.

SUN

Of all things, sunshine is taken for granted the most.

On a sunny day no one stops to ask:
Why is the apple sweet?
Or cherry blossoms pink?

Yet the sun knows.

THE GAZELLE HOP

It wasn't the runners' high, but the gazelle's hop.
I wasn't running, but my dreams were carrying me.

Like some kind of spiritual dance
I was suspended between man and medium,

Home and Away.

I heard ancestors sending encouragement
Even my totem, the elephant, was trumpeting.
So, I hopped
Like a gazelle across the Savannah
Away from home.

IRENE'S PRAYER

Crackling in the distance is a fire
The flames dance like African mermaids
The heat warms my soul and my belly is full
The demons lay at bay tonight
The kind that live only in my head
There is a silence both around me and inside of me
Some call it peace.

Around this ancient fire, something is missing
I remember my mother, aunt, and siblings around a
    similar fire
My aunt Irene always knew how to make a good fire
    and recite a prayer
What I would do to be around that fire tonight with her
Somewhere in Zimbabwe, Irene sits around a fire alone
The laughter of kids is only in her head
A situation every old person knows too well
Maybe an African folktale will fill her emptiness?
Perhaps roasted maize will satisfy her hunger to see her kids?

She is a grandmother now
But some of her grandkids only exist in name; she has
never seen them
Will she ever see my kids?

Her vision is failing her, but not her memory
Old age has taught her that only god can keep the
    family safe
So, before she goes to bed, she sends a prayer in her
    customary way
From oldest to youngest.

Tonight, we all sleep in peace
Because Irene prayed
Nothing consoles the longing of family like a prayer
before bed.

SECTION TWO

BUILDING A LIFE IN AMERICA

JOURNEY

How did I ever come to this land?
To pick up and go into the unknown
One suitcase
Some faith and hope
Alone I ventured
On this road meant for me alone
To travel to these great lengths.

PROCESS

Process is more valuable than result
Like life and death.

A breathing being
is a process with mistakes and luck.

Result is death
No more change but the end
Devoid of the splendor of surprises.

Try not to predict the future
Discern it!
Love not the end but the process
and enjoy the secret of life.

SPIRITUALITY

A parched piece of land
Barren of any fruits
A dried up river
Void of the wonders of the sea
A dark chamber
No light can enter
A bland dish
Lacking the taste of spices
A dull day
Deprived of color and wonder
A lack of spirituality!

HOLY

To sit alone in silence is holy.
Resist the temptation of doing.

This is not idle time,
The mind never sleeps.

Assume not
its ever presence!

Soon to be replaced by life's trifles
Work, or other engagement
Maybe children
Their shrieks and laughter.

Idleness
Now a longing for past time

So many great things in life
They pass you while you are doing – what?

PAWNS

There was so much CHANGE in this one place
They boasted about it.
There was so much CHANGE in this one place
They were addicted.
There was so much CHANGE in this one place
Nothing really changed.
There was so much CHANGE in this one place
That I left.
There was so much CHANGE in this one place
And none of it was meant for us
None of it was meant for pawns.

RICE WITHOUT RIGHTS

Rice without rights,
Never take one without the other.

Without rice starvation abounds,
Without rights poison seeps.

State of America!
Rice without rights.

Or is it corn?

Poison creeps in my belly with every bite,
Suffocating my veins with sugar.

Death from within.
Rice without rights.

HUMANS

An internal conflict,
A type of civil war!

Friendly fire!
A self-defeating process.

Ever repeating itself,
Generation after generation.

A cancerous race!
Fathered wars,

Birthed global warming,
Invented poverty.

Forever divided!
Marching slowly to its death.

Humans!

LITTLE LEOPARDS

Little leopards grow and when they grow, they bite.
Once a harmless remark
Brushed aside as cute.
Maybe a joke.
A little leopard!
Surprisingly grew.
Turned into a passion,
Fueled with conviction.
Ready to pounce and devour.
A grown leopard.
Racist!
Sexist!
Homophobe!
Was once a little leopard.

NIGGA, HOMO, CRACKER, DYKE

What do you think calling me a nigga would change?
Or calling me a cracker would change?
Or dyke or homo or whatever you choose?
Do I suddenly become smaller?
Crumbling with fear from your name calling?
Do you become bigger, stronger, all powerful?
Exalted and majestic from the names you call out
Don't you know that the only thing that lasts
Is what I call myself in my head
And it's not nigga, homo, cracker, or dyke!

BOOKS AND COVERS

We met him on a lake
He had a large offensive belly and wore star spangled
    shorts
Country music blasted through the air.

I'm black and he was white
History taught me to listen and fear these signs.

History is complicated
His kindness pierced through my prejudices
Never judge a book by its cover.

ALONG THE WAY

Somewhere along the way, you realized it's not enough
   anymore.
It was an idle Tuesday, I was lazily staring through the
   window
Suddenly I was awake to the moment and came to
   a realization
The accolades don't carry the same flattery
The extra dollar has lost its weight
The enthusiasm has turned into anxiety
Only the Shonas know how to describe it: "Aiva Madziva
   Ava Mazambuko."

I look back and it was once a beautiful road but I can't lie
   to myself anymore
Everything has changed!
While I have done well for myself, I also have lost part
   of me
I remember how I used to desire this thing, this job
   and that . . .
But today it becomes clearer
I am ready to be a father.

AT FIRST, I HAD
ONLY QUESTIONS

Are kids some kind of panacea?
A necessary medicine to a meaningless life?
Do they complete us?
Maybe enhance us?
Do they restore joy and direction?
Are they a true measure of success?
An extension of a legacy?
Do they become a fountain of hope?
A sanctuary?
A partial copy of who we are?
Do we see ourselves in them
As roles reverse?
Do they make death easier
Knowing part of us continues to live?

LOVE

Once, it happened to me.
In silence, I felt it
Drawing me out
Neither gentle nor rough
Just a perfect balance!
A yearning to be part of something
I had resisted.
A cold resistance, hardened by the hypocrisy of the world.
Then it happened,
Unknowingly and effortlessly
Melting my inner nature.
I let go and dove,
Plunging to the bottom of Victoria Falls.
Landed in her arms
With no explanation I understood.
I was crazy.
I was in love.

TSVARAKADENGA

Acts of kindness.

From the small hand-sewn Aztec gifts
To the dark aroma of Monteverde coffee,
And the red tinge of Pinotage

From time spent feeding the homeless
And time spent at home with the restless

From remembering a scarf
To small hand-written cards

Like Chichén Itza and Zambezi
You are a Fortress with grace.
In this garden of Eden
You are the gift.

MUD POOLS

Environment is conducive to success
One cannot swim in a mud pool.

To grow one has to be in a growing environment,
the tide that raises all boats.

Many men failed to reach great heights
Not for lack of skill but environment.

Change your environment change your luck.
My luck changed in America.

SECTION THREE

TRAVELING
AROUND
THE WORLD

TRAVEL

My two happiest states:
just before leaving and about to return

Anticipation fuels the happiness before
But reality rarely lives up

Once it might happen
A trip of a lifetime

A momentary glimpse of happiness
Perhaps an activity

Some delicacy
Or a kind stranger

I bag some of this joy and vow to take it back home
It doesn't take long to see the cracks

Novelty wears off
I am dreaming of the first place I wanted to leave

Maybe the feeling of my cozy bed,
Or a story to tell

I crave them, not because they are better but because
    they are mine
My home

With new eyes, I feel grateful
The mundane is now a luxury

Happy memories:
Day by day I relive them, and excitement builds up

With more time passing, I am ready to start all over again
Maybe to bring back some joy

Or to be reminded of all the goodness at home
Traveling is only great when you have a home to return to.

EN LA CALLE

A pregnant street
Bursting with silence
Awaiting birth!

"Caminando y Tomando"

A slice of heaven
Sandwiched between hell
Awaiting judgment

"Caminando y Comiendo"

A tight string
Pulled on both ends
Waiting to break

"Caminando y Pensando"

A bleeding pen
Drop by drop
Bleeding to death

"Caminando y Escribiendo"

It had been 5 years since I wrote poems.
In that street, I started writing again.

AWAY

I can lose you to another man,
But never lose the friendship we built.

I can miss your warm body besides me,
But never forget the warm feeling in my heart!

I can stop seeing you every day
But never erase the fond memories we shared.

I can forget what it means to talk to you every day
But never forget your smile.

Even if we are physically separated, we are eternally linked.
Somebody lied to me:

Separation, death, break-ups—
Where is the pain you promised?

Even sadness is enjoyable, if given its time.

SIMPLY

A walk along the beach,
Simply relaxing.
A bite into fruit,
Simply delicious.
An honest hug,
Simply warm.
A cracking laughter,
Simply contagious.
A sweaty exercise,
Simply refreshing.
An old story,
Simply magical.
A genuine smile,
Simply affectionate.
Why search for complexity?
The joys in life are in simplicity!

IN FLORENCE

In the land of gods,
David towered over them all,
Firenze!
Arno whispered silent secrets
Eyes cried from beauty
Time stopped!
Ears heard Michelangelo's stones shouting:
Art is God,
God is Art!

IMMORTALS

Siblings suckling from the same breast:
Musicians and Poets.

If art is God
Who then are his messengers?

With word and song
Laughter and sorrow
The future and past greet each other.

What greater calling is there in life,
but to be a Poet or Musician?

STRANGERS

We met a man when we were drinking port
He was short but talked tall
He knew more about Africa than I did
Ever heard of São Tomé and Príncipe?
It was like talking to an uncle with the spirit of Fado.

An Andalusian gave me two bananas; we had no change.
Another one poured Tinto de Verano with such humility,
    it felt like my mama's kitchen.

An English waitress returned a 20 Euro we'd dropped,
    while offering us port
like a childhood friend.

Loving-kindness they all possess:
I had to write these words down, lest I forget
the strangers whose perfect smiles brightened the days.
I had never met them before, but I had known them
    my whole life.

CALM

I.

A gradual silence comes over me
Slowly it draws me in, caressing my soul

I can hear my heart beat
Thump thump thump

There is nothingness
As I drink deeply, each breath

I let go slowly, while absence cleans my soul
Everything is reduced to this absence

There is neither before nor after
I don't want to leave
This sacred moment

Like a thief in the night, they arrive
Like a river gushing, multitudes of thoughts ambush me
They have stolen and battered my peace

An ending to my meditation
Being calm is a skill worth pursuing.

II.
A calm mind is not a silent one
Focus is not the absence of distractions.

Through chatters and impulses
It holds still.

Seeing and Listening
Yet, it does not act.

Like a mountain
It endures all seasons.

A calm mind is one that observes everything
And remains unchanged.

LUXURY & NIGHTMARES

100°F stuck on a highway in the desert
Sweat trickled down every crevice of my body
The car had broken down!
Our driver apologized!
In his eyes, I saw it.
It broke my heart.
A sincere apology!
Our luxury is someone's nightmare, when unmet.
Such a realization changes you!

GRATITUDE

My soul is a river of gratitude.
Never ending,

Ever flowing.
Both in the deep and the shallow,

cheery and dreary.
Who to thank: God or Man?

Error in the question
Deems the answer obsolete.

Empathy is gratitude
To see cheery in the Dreary,

And dreary in the Cheery.
'Tis hidden in gratitude, that we find the rarest form
    of happiness.

TIME AND MONEY

Twins fought from birth
Fists thrown from opposite ends

Time and Money!
Fighting for our attention

First, we had time and no money: we were young!
And then money and no time: we are old!

The equation of life is balanced by time and money
So, I booked the hot air balloon flight

Time and Money permitted.

IMMIGRANT

Who knew there were immigrants in Cappadocia?
He looked Turkish but he was Afghan

There is a story behind every sorrowful face
Right then, I understood the war

Immigrants live on hope and memory
A diet I know very well.

Like him, we will never forget where we came from.

AT THE TURKISH BATHS

Generous smiles were offered through crooked teeth!
One scrubbed my back,
The other poured oil in my hair,
Hammam!
It was his first time touching my kind of hair
It is easier to hate people from the news
It is much easier to love them in person
Lord help me remember this!

SUNRISE

Every ending is another beginning.

Sunrises over sunsets!
I prefer beginnings over endings.

This calm is expensive and expansive all around
The air is crisp and life cleansing.

A lonely bird sings solemnly
I prefer being alone than in a crowd.

The sun breaks
The possibilities are numerous
at sunrise.

MIRACLES

God, Destiny, or the Universe
Many times, knows what you need before you do
In secret, works on it, without your knowledge
Rearranging life
Things work out, without your noticing
And happily, your life moves on
To be lucky is to stop once in a while
And observe these miracles around you.

AFTERWORD

NOTES

Some things are best written and not spoken out loud. And history not captured, curses the future. This book is a connection between my past and my future. I wrote these poems over a span of 15 years, and offer them now to my family: the family who raised me and the family I hope to raise. For the family I hope to start, I hope these will be a way for you to know my life before you, and for you to celebrate and lay claim to our shared history and culture. And for my mother, aunts, and my sisters: I wrote these poems in gratitude for your love, without which I would not be the man I am. I hope you can return to this book over and over again. There is no particular preferred order to read the book (although we tried to establish an order). When in love, read poems about love; when you want to understand African culture, read the section on growing up in Africa; when dealing with death, read poems about death; when traveling, read poems about traveling and so forth. To my other readers, I hope you will take the time to "Reflect" as you read this book.

To learn more about the author: www.itaidavidnjanji.com

REFERENCES

Imagery and Places:
All poems are influenced by real life experiences. There is
no better source of inspiration than life. There is a lot of
imagery and names of places in all poems. I encourage readers to take their time, reviewing the places and imagery to
fully understand the spirit of the poems. In all cases, the
"Travel" poems section was written while traveling in the
place that is referenced.

En la Calle:
This poem was written on the streets of Sevilla, Spain. "En
la Calle" means "on the street" in Spanish. I can commu-
nicate in three languages (Shona, English, and Spanish) and
this is reflected in some of the poems. I was walking a lot
in Europe (~ 5-7 miles a day) and that is when I started
writing poems again after 5 years. Most ideas came to me
during these walks. Key Spanish phrases in this poem are:
"Caminando y Comiendo," "Walking and Eating;" "Caminando y Tomando," "Walking and Drinking;" Caminando y
"Pensando," "Walking and Thinking;" "Caminando y Escribiendo," "Walking and Writing". These words describe the
writing experience during that trip.

Tsvarakadenga:
This poem is about love. I am describing a woman. I
changed the title of the poem many times as neither an
English or Spanish word could fully describe the essence of
the poem. I settled on this Shona word, which describes a

beautiful woman. But the meaning in Shona is much deeper than beauty in its normal sense (physical, intellectual etc.). Tsvarakadenga is never lightly used in Shona.

Along the Way:
This poem describes the changes of life and in my case, culminating to my desire to become a father. This phenomenon is accurately expressed with a Shona idiom: "Aiva Madziva Ava Mazambuko." This means, "What was once a river is now a bridge". This idiom can be said differently as well: "Aiva Mazambuko Ava Madziva". I feel lucky to have these languages to pick and choose the best one to describe a phenomenon that is so close to my heart.

ACKNOWLEDGMENTS

- Megan Snyder-Camp, thank you for copy editing this book with clarity.
- Jess LaGreca, thank you for all the designs that make this book a work of art.
  Learn more: jesslagreca.com
- MK Williams, thank you for your counsel, without which this book would not have been published.
  Learn more: 1mkwilliams.com